First World War
and Army of Occupation
War Diary
France, Belgium and Germany

4 CAVALRY DIVISION
Divisional Troops
Royal Army Service Corps
Divisional Ammunition Park (79 Company A.S.C.)
14 March 1916 - 12 December 1917

WO95/1158/12

The Naval & Military Press Ltd
www.nmarchive.com
Published in association with The National Archives

Published by

The Naval & Military Press Ltd

Unit 10 Ridgewood Industrial Park,

Uckfield, East Sussex,

TN22 5QE England

Tel: +44 (0) 1825 749494

www.naval-military-press.com

www.nmarchive.com

This diary has been reprinted in facsimile from the original. Any imperfections are inevitably reproduced and the quality may fall short of modern type and cartographic standards.

© Crown Copyright
Images reproduced by permission of The National Archives, London, England, 2015.

Contents

Document type	Place/Title	Date From	Date To
Heading	WO95/1158/12		
Heading	4th Cav Div Troops 4th Cav Div Amms Park (late 1st Ind Cav Div) (79 Coy ASC) 1916 Oct-1917 Dec To GHQ Troops Box 135		
Heading	War Diary of Ammunition Park 4th Cavalry Division (Late 1st I.C Divn) From 1st October 1916 To 30th November 1916		
War Diary	Labroye	01/10/1916	31/10/1916
Heading	War Diary of 4th Cavalry Divisional Ammunition Park		
War Diary	Labroye	01/11/1916	02/11/1916
War Diary	Pinchefalise	03/11/1916	29/11/1916
War Diary	In the Field	30/11/1916	30/11/1916
Heading	War Diary of Ammunition Park 4th Cavalry Division From 1st December 1916 To 31st December 1916		
War Diary	In the Field	01/12/1916	11/12/1916
War Diary	Pinchefalise	11/12/1916	13/12/1916
War Diary	Pontremy	14/03/1916	14/03/1916
War Diary	Pinchefalise	15/12/1916	31/12/1916
Heading	War Diary of 4th Cavalry Divisional Ammunition Park. from 1st January 1917 To 31st January 1917		
War Diary	Pinchefalise	01/01/1917	31/01/1917
Heading	War Diary of 4th Cavalry Divisional Ammunition Park For Month of February 1917		
War Diary	Pinchefalise	01/02/1917	28/02/1917
Heading	War Diary of 4th Cavalry Divisional Ammunition Farm For Month Of March 1917		
War Diary	Pinchefalise	01/03/1917	23/03/1917
War Diary	Field	24/03/1917	31/03/1917
Heading	War Diary of 4th Cavalry Divisional Ammunition Park For Month of April 1917		
War Diary	Field	01/04/1917	30/04/1917
Heading	War Diary For Month Ending May-17 4th Cav. Div. Amm. Park from 1st may to 30th June 1917		
War Diary	Field	01/05/1917	31/05/1917
Heading	War Diary For June 1917 4th Cavalry Divisional Ammunition Park For June 1917		
War Diary	Field	01/06/1917	30/06/1917
Heading	War Diary. 4th Cav Divl Ammtn Park July 1917		
War Diary	Field	01/07/1917	31/07/1917
Heading	War Diary For August 1917 4th Cavalry Divisional Ammunition Park August 1917		
War Diary	Le Mesnil	01/08/1917	31/08/1917
Heading	War Diary for September 1917		
War Diary	Le Mesnil	01/09/1917	13/09/1917
War Diary	Field	13/09/1917	26/09/1917
War Diary	In the Field	27/09/1917	30/09/1917
Heading	War Diary for October 1917 4th Cavalry Divisional Ammunition Park.		
War Diary	In the Field	01/10/1917	31/10/1917

Heading	War Diary of 4th Cavalry Divisional Ammunition Park For November 1917		
War Diary	Field	01/11/1917	30/11/1917
Heading	War Diary of 4th Cavalry Divisional Ammn Park For December 1917		
War Diary	Field O.8 d 6.2 Shut 62. C	01/12/1917	06/12/1917
War Diary	Field	07/12/1917	12/12/1917

WO 95/11581/2

4th Cav Div Troops

4th Cav Div Ammo Park
(late 1st Ind Cav Div)

(79 Coy ASC)

1916 OCT — 1917 DEC

TO GHQ TROOPS BOX 135

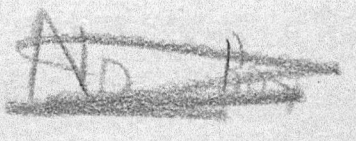

SERIAL NO. 146.

4th Cav. Div. Train

Confidential
War Diary
of

Ammunition Park, 4th Cavalry Division. (late 1st I.C. Div.)

FROM 1st October 1916 TO 30th November 1916.
~~1st October~~ ~~1916~~

Army Form C. 2118.

WAR DIARY
or
INTELLIGENCE SUMMARY.
(Erase heading not required.)

Place	Date	Hour	Summary of Events and Information	Remarks and references to Appendices
LA BROYE	1.10.16	-	Usual Routine	
"	2.10.16	-	Usual Routine. Inspection of horses	
"	3.10.16	12.15	Relieved 222 MG Coy of Watch. L/Cpl Smith + 2 men + 2 Plumes	
"	4.10.16	-	Burying to O.C. 7th Battalion for company orderly. A/Lt Knight + 12 OR's 4/4/16	
"	5.10.16	10 am	" L/Cpl Watson + party on Transport OR's. A/Lt Knight IC WTB 4/4/16	
"	6.10.16	-	Inspection from 1st Army HQ. Usual Routine	
"	7.10.16	3 pm	Orderly L/Cpl Evans to Det train Cdn Artillery 12 NSE — 2nd Engineer skin 2 wm NS 2 pm by	
"	"	"	M/C State 20 Lewis Safety bags 720 Lewis Mil Res Pouches. Received from Quartermr Colin 56 Primers (Type MS 23)	
"	"	"	Amn S.A.A. SC.fd.S.30 2/5/1/6	
"	8.10.16	-	Inspection of Artillery now Clothing Returns	
"	9.10.16	2-10p	Chief Inst W.A.D.Court Inquiry to Det Hune OR requisitions + Kit list	
"	10.10.16	-	Usual Routine	
"	11.10.16	11 am	Burying Capt Blake to HUA LE CHATEAU to have mate Regd to 35 Toch Horse 3rd	
"	"	-	MO Sgt 12 Grenade will NUS + Gun Cotton Charges etc	
"	12.10.16	2 pm	Capt Ainslie L/Cpl Young + 2 OR's to BOULOGNE. Bringing to & from to Det Ammn Col 2 Bx MG Ch	
"	"	-	Amn S.A.A. 432 Hand Grad 13 Verey Shell 12 Gun Cotton Charges to Q.Ordnance. 1st Divisional	

WAR DIARY or INTELLIGENCE SUMMARY

Army Form C. 2118.

18

Place	Date	Hour	Summary of Events and Information	Remarks and references to Appendices
LA BROYE	13.10.16	7.45am	Four Lorries Sergt Blair A.S.C. to LIEGESCOURT to report to D.A.D.O.S. for duty.	ASC
"	14.10.16		Selected to Divisional Ammunition Column 4000 rds S.A.A. 1980 rds Rifle Wallets 784 Grenades No 5	ASC
"	15.10.16		One Lorry 1/c 2nd Cpl Adams to Div.l Ammunition Colm with 4000 rds SAA 100 rds Shrapnel & 150 Cartge Shun? Inspection of Lorries. Car to BOULOGNE to report to Lieut Col Charlton R.H.A. and bring him back to his quarters. Church Parade at 5 pm in conjunction with A Battery RHA and Divisional Supply Column	ASC
"	16.10.16	7.45am	Two Lorries 1/c Sergt Hall to LIEGESCOURT to report for duty to D.A.D.O.S.	ASC
"	17.10.16	" "	Two Lorries 1/c Sergt Short ASC to LIEGESCOURT for duty under orders of D.A.D.O.S.	ASC
"	" "		Car to Div.l Ammunition Colm to return 287 Grenades No 5 (drills) & Three defect. thyr No 11 & 50 Mills digits	ASC
"	18.10.16	" "	Two Lorries 1/c Sergt Blair A.S.C. to LIEGESCOURT to report to DADOS for duty. All grenades cleaned with paraffin.	ASC
"	19.10.16	11.30am	Four Lorries 1/c Sergt Galliven ASC to Railhead to report to representative of DADOS for duty	ASC
"	" "	4 pm	One Lorry 1/c L. Cpl. Clark ASC to CAUMARTIN to report to O.C. 29th Lancers to return 25 tents	ASC
"	" "	6 pm	No 1 Section 1/c 2/Lt RSC Wood ASC with 2/Lt J.E. Stacey R.F.A. consisting of 15 Lorries and carrying 616 rds H.E. and 1886 rds Shrapnel detached and proceeded to HAVERNAS to join 1st Cavalry Division Ammunition Park. Vide Authority Q 4232 of 19/10/16.	ASC

WAR DIARY or INTELLIGENCE SUMMARY

Army Form C. 2118.

Place	Date	Hour	Summary of Events and Information	Remarks and references to Appendices
LABROYE	20.10.16	—	Usual routine. Inspection of clothing and issue of shirts	
"	21.10.16	6 am	Tushance /o Sgt Stour ASC to report to O.C. RE Stores @ ABANCOURT and to there and deliver certain timber to REQUIERE EGLISE	M/C
"	"	7 "	Tushance to Sgt Till ASC with L/Cpl Peacock RE to RE dumps South of towards ALBERT. An indicates by L/Cpl Peacock to pick up stores and deliver same at REQUIERE EGLISE	M/C
"	"	7.30 "	Guduray /o L/Cpl Clark ASC to LE CAUROY Airport to representative of DAD.OS for duty under his direction	M/C
"	"	"	Dumped all ammunition in order to complywith Approximate 14 tons Movement for	M/C
"	22.10.16	9.30am	14 Lorries /o 2/Lt R.O. Cooke ASC after collecting Machine Gun Squadrons of Sialkot & Mhow Brigades to SAILLY AU BOIS via DOULLENS PAS & SOUASTRE The Party were landed at COIGNEUX according to orders of Town Major SAILLY AU BOIS	M/C
"	"	5 pm	No.1 (Can) Section /o 2/Lt Stracey R.F.A. returned and reported Park	
"	23.10.16	9.30am	Tushance /o L/Cpl Hannar ASC to MONDICOURT to collect RE stores from RE Park to deliver same to various units of Brigadier	R/C
"	"	11.30am	One Lorry /o L/Cpl Osborne ASC to Q Battery RHA Ambulance Bearer A 4300 ALS HX	

WAR DIARY
INTELLIGENCE SUMMARY

Army Form C. 2118.

Place	Date	Hour	Summary of Events and Information	Remarks and references to Appendices
LA BROYE	24/10/16	7 a.m.	8 Lorries & S/Sgt Cullen A.S.C. with fatigue party of 1 NCO & 8 men to LE CAUROY to lift and transfer stores from Salvage Dump to HOINCOURT and to remain the night and return on the morning after completing duty. (Authority Q 439 d/23.x.16.)	
"	25.10.16	6 a.m.	One Lorry & S/Sgt Blair A.S.C. to LE CAUROY to lift stores from Divisional dumps & return to HOINCOURT (Authority AT.M.C. HOC 20/55 d/24.x.16)	
"	"	7 a.m.	One lorry & L/Cpl Foster R.E. to MARCHEVILLE to carry party to Cpl Copse R.E. (The whole of lorries & fatigues necessitated by move being sent to WOINCOURT)	
"	26.10.16	9 a.m.	Two lorries & Cpl Hearne to MONDICOURT to collect salvage stores to HOINCOURT — 1st lorry under Cpl Hearne & Rifle Foster Smith to BOISMONT to continue daily duty under Field Squadron	
"	"	8 a.m.	Four lorries & Sergt Scott A.S.C. to BEAURAINVILLE for duty under orders of representative of DADOS	
"	27.10.16	6.30 a.m.	Two lorries & Cpl Vinian to LE CAUROY with NCO & Field Squadron borrowing dumps	
"	"	9 a.m.	One lorry & L/Cpl Clark to LIGESCOURT for duty under orders of DADOS	
"	"		Three lorries & Sergt Cullen ASC to BEAURAINVILLE for duty under orders of DADOS	
"	28.10.16	—	Usual routine	
"	29.10.16	9.15 a.m.	One lorry & L/Cpl Adams & No 5 RE dumps @ MONDICOURT and thence to Steele Dump & deliver stores	
"	30.10.16	—	Usual routine	

Army Form C. 2118.

WAR DIARY
or
INTELLIGENCE SUMMARY

(Erase heading not required.)

Instructions regarding War Diaries and Intelligence Summaries are contained in F. S. Regs., Part II. and the Staff Manual respectively. Title pages will be prepared in manuscript.

Place	Date	Hour	Summary of Events and Information	Remarks and references to Appendices
LA GORGUE	31.10.16	10 A.M.	Inspection of blankets & smoke helmets tins of the latter returned to store partition issued in exchange. Five horses standing by for Corps H.Q. Auth. P. & Q 3872/29/AQ) 2.10.16	

H.M. Howard
Capt.
OC 1st Indian Cavalry Divl Ammunition Park

[stamp: 79 (M.T.) Co. A.S.C. FINTRY PARK 31/10/16]

Army Form C. 2118

WAR DIARY
or
INTELLIGENCE SUMMARY
(Erase heading not required.)

Instructions regarding War Diaries and Intelligence Summaries are contained in F. S. Regs., Part II. and the Staff Manual respectively. Title Pages will be prepared in manuscript.

WAR DIARY

OF

4th CAVALRY DIVISIONAL AMMUNITION PARK.

H.R. Hornby Captain
a/o
& 4th Cavalry Divisional Ammunition Park

Place	Date	Hour	Summary of Events and Information	Remarks and references to Appendices

WAR DIARY
INTELLIGENCE SUMMARY

Place	Date	Hour	Summary of Events and Information	Remarks and references to Appendices
LACROYE	1916 May 1	7 am	Three lorries & Sgt Bell A.S.C. to MADICOURT to report to O.C. Ambulances. Three lorries & Cpl Cullen A.S.C. to ESTREE WAMIN to report to OC 32 CCS	
"	"	7.20 am	Ordinary & Cpl Clark ASC to RAYE SUR AUTHIE to report to OC Ambulance	
"	"	"	Two lorries & L/Cpl Hamilton RSC to DOURIEZ to report to OC 39 CCS	
"	"	7.30 am	Ordinary & L/Cpl Adams ASC to DOURIEZ to report to 3.30 MAC & on return	
"	"	8.30 am	Two lorries & Cpl HEARNE ASC to report to OC Machine Gun Squadron M&SV Offr at LACROYE	
"	"		Ulcher ambulances after loading to rendezvous at CANCHY and proceed to rendez of B.S.O. to rest billeting area immediately be reported returning to PREAUX	
"	"	1 pm	Ordinary & L/Cpl Sneddon ASC to LIGESCOURT for duty under orders of B.S.O.	
"	"	"	Ordinary & L/Cpl Watson ASC to MONDICOURT to load ready RE stores thence to BOISMONT	
"	"	"	One Lorry & Pte Nash ASC to S/Sgt Ammunition Column Killeen 33000 and last journal at 1st Churchill valle	
"	2	5 am	Ordinary & AC Holland ASC to St PREAUX (ready under orders of Supply Officer STALHOT 1300s	

Army Form C. 2118.

WAR DIARY
or
INTELLIGENCE SUMMARY.
(Erase heading not required.)

Place	Date	Hour	Summary of Events and Information	Remarks and references to Appendices
LABROYE	2 Nov 16	5 am	On duty 1/c Pte Barton ASC to CRECY for duty under orders of B.S.O LUCKNOW B/DE	
"	"	12.30 pm	Five lorries 1/c Sergt Blair ASC to neallies (BEAURAINVILLE) and to proceed thence as ordered by R.S.O.	MSC
" "	"	2 pm	Three lorries to PINCHEFALISE 1/c Cpl Lord ASC for duty there tomorrow as below	
PINCHEFALISE	3 Nov 16	7.30 am	One lorry to WOINCOURT to draw rations	
"	"	"	Two lorries 1/c L/Cpl Adams ASC to BOISMONT 16 report (in adv) to F.O.C. Field Squadron	
"	"	1 PM	Three lorries 1/c 2/Lieut Ward RE arrived from LABROYE in advance of Park to make arrangements for parking vehicles	
"	"	2 pm	Remainder of Park arrived. Park 5 lorries 1/c Sergt Blair which had returned arrived and parked in village on STANLEY road	MSC
"	"	7 pm	Runaway Gun lorries 1/c 2/Lieut Cooke ASC who had remained behind from LABROYE to attend to and clean of letters arrived and rate 2/Lt Stacey RFA who had remained to supervise loading of ammunition changed pushed back	
"	4 Nov 16	6.45 am	On duty 1/c Lce Cpl Watson to report for duty to O.C. Field Squadron at BELLOY	
"	"	7.40 am	Two lorries Cpl Hawkins to report for duty to F.O.E. Field Squadron at BOISMONT	MSC
"	5 Nov 16	6.15 am	On duty 1/c Lce Cpl Watson to report for duty to OC Troop RE at BELLOY	

WAR DIARY or INTELLIGENCE SUMMARY

Army Form C. 2118.

Place	Date	Hour	Summary of Events and Information	Remarks and references to Appendices
ANCRE VILLE	5/Nov	7.40am	One horse h/c Pte Starke to report to O.C. Field Squadron at BOISMONT. Spare men return...	ADSS
"	"	"	Two horses h/c L/Cpl Stahn(?) Smith to report to O.C. Field Squadron at BOISMONT. Spare men returning to MONDICOURT	
"	"	9.35am	Ten horses h/c 2/Lt Hunt RSC to report to B.G. LUCKNOW BDE at (half way(?) mile N.E of FOREST L'ABBAYE to hand over spare horses - Five horses to return to B&O LUCKNOW BDE at MOYENVILLE. Nine to SIALKOTE BDE at PENDE. Two to R.O.D.T. at PRESSEYVILLE and two to B&O MHOW BDE at BELLOY	ADSS
"	6 Nov	7.40am	Two horses h/c L/Cpl Hamilton to BOISMONT to report to O.C. Field Squadron for duty	ADSS
"	"	10am	Two horses h/c Cpl Hanna h/c to Cpl PREAUX to collect coal from Dump 1 Picket Brigade and delivere same at PENDE	
"	7 Nov	6.45am	One horse h/c H/Cpl Watson to BELLOY to report to O.C. Field Troop RE for duty with him	
"	"	7am	One horse h/c L/Cpl Davidson to BOISMONT to report for duty to O.C. Field Squadron	
"	"	9.45am	Ten horses h/c 2/Lt Curtis ASC to report ½ mile N.E of FOREST L'ADDAYE to meet B&O LUCKNOW BDE to hand over - Two horses to deliver to SQDT PRESSEYVILLE, Two to B&O MHOW BDE at BELLOY, One to B&O LUCKNOW BDE at MOYENVILLE & having part Three to B&O SIALKOT BDE @ PENDE and three to B&O LUCKNOW BDE at MOYENVILLE & having part	ADSS

Army Form C. 2118.

WAR DIARY
or
INTELLIGENCE SUMMARY.
(Erase heading not required.)

Place	Date	Hour	Summary of Events and Information	Remarks and references to Appendices
PONCHEVALISE	7.11.16	—	10 gunners accompanied the horses but owing to shortness of forward (Batm?) from road of the important lorry party. The lorry was not complete till 4.15 pm and sorry of the lorries did not return till 10 pm	
"	8.11.16	7.40am	One lorry 1/c L/Cpl Selby to BOISMONT for duty with OC Field Squadron RE	
"	9.11.16	"	One lorry " "	
"	"	8.15 "	One lorry 1/c Pte Ellis to FRIVILLE to report for duty to OC Field Squadron	
"	"	9 am	One lorry 1/c L/Cpl Foster Smith to ARQUES and thence to MONS BOUBERT milk stores	
"	10.11.16	6.45am	One lorry 1/c L/Cpl Watson to FRIVILLE to report for duty to RE representative	
"	"	7.40 "	Two lorries 1/c A Pte Mortimer & Farnham respectively to BOISMONT for OC Field Squadron	
"	"	7.45 "	One lorry 1/c L/Cpl Jewett to BOISMONT and thence to RE Park MONDICOURT	
"	"	4 pm	Two lorries 1/c L/Cpl Foster Smith to report for duty to OC Supply Depot ABBEVILLE and thence to MOYENNEVILLE	
"	11.XI.16	6.30am	Two lorries 1/c Sgt Gullivan to ORmericourt Dump WOINCOURT & thence independently to deliver stores	
"	"	7.15 "	One lorry 1/c Pte Ellis to Divisional Station FRIVILLE	
"	"	7.40 "	Two lorries 1/c Cpl Hearn to BOISMONT to report for duty to OC Field Squadron	
"	12.XI.16	"	One lorry 1/c L/Cpl Foster Smith to BOISMONT to report to OC Field Squadron & thence to MONDICOURT	

WAR DIARY or INTELLIGENCE SUMMARY

Army Form C. 2118.

Place	Date	Hour	Summary of Events and Information	Remarks and references to Appendices
PINCHEFALISE	13.XI.16	7.15am	One Lorry i/c Pte Ellis to FRIVILLE to report for duty to O.C. Field Squadron	
"	14.11	7.30 "	" " i/c L/Cpl Hunter Smith to WOINCOURT station for duty under orders of O.C. R.E. Field Squadron	
"	" "	" "	Six lorries i/c Sgt Stott to report at Divisional Dumps PRESSEUXVILLE and carry hay to Supply Depot at ST VALERY	
"	" "	8.40 "	One lorry i/c Pte Newhouse to BOISMONT to report for duty to O.C. Field Squadron R.E.	
"	" "	11.4m	Eight lorries of unit by L/Cpl Snow O.C. A.S.C. to Jackin. Owing to weather	
"	" "	5pm	Ten lorries i/c 2/Lt R.B. Cooke to PRESSEUXVILLE to report to D.O. Divisional Supply Column for duty to load and proceed with so lorries of K.B.S.C. to CREST to CRECY Forest to load Wood and afterwards deliver same to Supply Officer of Division according to orders from HQ 18 Divn	
"	15.XI.16	8 am	35.181 14.11.16	
"	" "	" "	One lorry to L/Cpl Hunter Smith to BOISMONT to report for duty with O.C. Fd Squadron	
"	16.XI.16	7.45am	Three lorries to Mr Hume " " " to report for duty to O.C.	
"	" "	" "	" i/c L/Cpl Hunter Smith to MONDICOURT "	
"	17.XI.16	6.10am	One lorry to Capt Hall Smith to BOISMONT to report to O.C. Field Squadron	
"	18.XI.16	"	Two lorries to L/Cpl Watson to BOISMONT " "	
"	" "	" "	Two Cars to S/M G.H. Pye SAA 1911 & Pike 1112 6.38 mm detto cartridges	
"	19.XI.16	" "	One lorry to L/Cpl Hunter Smith to BOISMONT	
"	" "	2.30pm	Six lorries (part of Sec D) i/c 2/Lt C. Wood detached and to BAUCOURT for Somme on march for	

Army Form C. 2118.

WAR DIARY
or
INTELLIGENCE SUMMARY.
(Erase heading not required.)

Place	Date	Hour	Summary of Events and Information	Remarks and references to Appendices
PICQUIGNY	19.11.14	2 p.m	FRANVILLERS six miles W. of ALBERT - "A" Batty. R.H.A. with section of Ammunition Column and Park having been temporarily attached to III Corps — and to report their X to O.C. III Corps Ammunition Park (Lieut Colonel) R.F.A. Bgde were A.1610 of 19/11/14	Nil
"	16.11.14	8.30 p/m	One lorry /c Sgt. Tull to FRESSENVILLERS to report to O.C. Brittons Column & there wait details of "U" Batty R.H.A. to L'ETOILE (actually 29 aug. R.D.S. 19.11.14)	Nil
"	20.11.14	7.1am	One lorry /c Pte Gibbard to BOISMONT to report for duty to O.C. Field Squadron	
"	"	8.10 "	" " " " to Lieut Adam " BOISMONT & thence to MONDICOURT and return to O.C. Field Squadron	Nil
"	"	10.45 "	" " " " to Le/Cpl Clark to St VALERY to report to O.C. Signal Squadron 1.2. and three	
"	"	" "	to Cavalry Corps H.Q. @ REGNIERE ECLUSE	
"	21.11.14	7.30 a.m	One lorry /c Pte Clifton to St VALERY to report for duty to O.C. Signals	Nil Spares
"	"	" "	Light Ambulance to BOISMONT " " " " " "	
"	"	8 "	" " Clark to St VALERY " " " " " "	
"	22.11.14	7.30am	" " Pte Salley to St VALERY " report for duty 15 O.C. Signals	
"	23.11.14	8 A.M	Three lorries to 1/Offr Hamilton to WOINCOURT to draw 150 boxes S.A.A. & various bombs grenades and miscellaneous explosives. Delivers to R.H. Training School 48 Grenades 10 to Lutte arms P. 275 Webley revolvers and to D.A.C. 20 R/fle Grenades No 23 and 100 Detonators No 8 Mark VII	Nil

2353 Wt. W2544/1454 700,000 5/15 D. D. & L. A.D.S.S./Forms/C. 2118.

Army Form C. 2118.

WAR DIARY
or
INTELLIGENCE SUMMARY.
(Erase heading not required.)

Instructions regarding War Diaries and Intelligence Summaries are contained in F. S. Regs., Part II. and the Staff Manual respectively. Title pages will be prepared in manuscript.

Place	Date	Hour	Summary of Events and Information	Remarks and references to Appendices
PONT REMY	24.XII.15	8 a.m.	Three lorries & 1 L/Cpl Adams & Boisimont transport for duty. R.O.S. Staff Inspection. Rifle Inspection	
"	25.XII.15	8 a.m.	One lorry & L/Cpl Humblett to Boismont (previously under orders) O.C. Field Section	B/C
"	26.XII.15	—	O.C. Visit to instruction attached to III Corps Ammunition Park. Party of 4 L/Cpl Woodruff	R/E
"	"	—	One lorry & L/Cpl Donaldson to Boismont. Three to Fressenneville to collect bricks	
"	27.XII.15	10 a.m.	One lorry & L/Cpl Adams to Abbeville. Left there ? & Escarbotin (Nixon BDE 4 P.M.)	R/E
"	"	"	One lorry & The Ox & O.C. Field Squadron at Boismont & 9 a.m. The lorry proceed to Mk 1 R.E Park Mondicourt to draw R.E Stores. Inspection of Quarters and Ammunition by O.C. 1st Ind R.H.A. Bde at 10 a.m. the improved training (by extract in? every thing is now)	
"	"	"	To inspect the 1st Indian Div Div Am'n Ho. There an H.Q. Car Divn and Ammunition Park in 4th Cav Div Am Park (Artillery) G.H.Q. No. 0 0/11835 d/24/11/15.)	
"	28/12/15	"	Inspection of lorries, harness, tools, Schedule, indenting slips, Field w 1st aid dressings and indoor dressings. Test Drive by O.C. of Car Det Amm Park at 11 a.m. Everything found in order. Roads covered w ice.	R/E
"	"	"	from 2.10 to 3.10 p.m. Rifle inspection & from at 4 p.m.	
"	29/12/15	"	One lorry to O.C. Signals, St Valery and Three & Fressenville. One lorry to Rocket movement. With Fatigue party of 20 non ranks a O.S at 7 a.m. Debris of explosive stores & Div Valoir at Cayeux.	R/E

Army Form C. 2118.

WAR DIARY
or
INTELLIGENCE SUMMARY.
(Erase heading not required.)

Instructions regarding War Diaries and Intelligence Summaries are contained in F. S. Regs., Part II. and the Staff Manual respectively. Title pages will be prepared in manuscript.

Place	Date	Hour	Summary of Events and Information	Remarks and references to Appendices
In the Field	30/4/16		Pte Henry to MISSEVILLE for duty. A/Sgt 17 Lawson to resume my Tour being Tuesday's 11. 21. 27/4/16. N.C.O. 4/2 Co. Div.) Lery returned 5.20 p.m. No M.T/12067.1 Corporal A.H. Clark 11.12. proceeded to G.H.Q. Troops Supply Column to be attached for the purpose of being tested as a sub Driver for a temporary Commission in the A.S.C. (authority A.D.S.T. Cavalry Corps No T/1157/a of 29/10/16. An Officer & Instructor delivered a Lecture at 11 a.m. in the Spare parts See field stores of the Unit from the 1st of April 1916 to date inclusive and the cost of same.	H.L.T.
	"			
	"			
	"			
	"			
	"			
	"			

W.H. Horne Captain
a/o
O.C. 4th Cavalry Divisional Ammunition Park.

79 (M.T) Co. A.S.C.
30/4/16
4TH CAV. DIV. AMMN. PARK

SERIAL NO. 146.

Confidential
War Diary
of

Ammunition Park, 4th Cavalry Division.

FROM 1st December 1916 TO 31st December 1916.

WAR DIARY or INTELLIGENCE SUMMARY

Army Form C. 2118.

(Erase heading not required.)

Place	Date	Hour	Summary of Events and Information	Remarks and references to Appendices
In the Field	1/12/16 2/12/16		Inspection of lorries & lorries by O.C. DAP. Everything in order.	Nil.
"	3.12.16		One lorry to CAYEUX Divisional School at 9am (4th Div) to move material. One lorry to Field Squadron R.E. at BOISMONT at 9am for carriage of stores. Inspection of general routine. No lorries on a scheme today.	Nil.
"	4.12.16		Advanced table of DAP at CONTAY was inspected by O.C.DAP. Everything being found to order. Route march under the Gunnery Officer.	Nil.
"	5.12.16		Party of 12 men on Command to Field Squadron R.E. for "fatigue work" in future — (1) 4 men lorry for about 4 days and (3) 8 men lorry for about 14 days. (Authority — NO.A. 1876 A/4/12/16 H.Q. of 4th Cav Div) One lorry to Field Squadron R.E. at 8am.	Nil.
"	6.12.16		One lorry to report to MHOW Bde H.Q. ESCARBOTIN at 8am tomorrow to pick up ordnance etc produced. The O.C. to report to H.Q.R. 14th K.D.G's (MIANWAY) the goods up that the arms are not to arrive (Authority on note form the ways to suggest) to be sending the lorry to the being in touch with representative. 1000 lbs weight while the lorries were to move from the goods to lorries & waived transport to a boarded representative on the dead weight.) The lorry sent the paperd to the proven Battalion & marked coveret to a boarded representative armed camp lorries & the return. MHOW camp lorries NO 13054 and returned the Railway Station (Authority 8.9760 6/12/16.) Railway Station took.	Nil.
"	7.12.16		One lorry to MHOW BDE H.Q. ESCARBOTIN at 12–11 fm to take a football team from MASSEVILLE and return (Authority OR.A.I.C. NO.R/9. 6/12/16.) Inspection of armament letter DAP in action (Authority OR.A.I.C. NO.R/9. 6/12/16. H.Q. Cav.Div.) Inspection of armament letter every DAP. The OR on found in order. One lorry to Dist. Ammunition Column this morning.	Nil.
"	8.12.16		Sgt Godden M.C. and his lorries proceeded at 7-30 am to CAYEUX, BRUTELLES, ARREST, CHEPY, CAHON, ABBEVILLE & carry 30 In & and the Railway Station. General routine.	Nil.
"	9.12.16		Usual routine. Inspection of lorries. Orderly I/c L/Cpl Chard to report to R.O.C. Spare Squadron (STABLERY) than in charge to and STYLELY. Usual weekly inspection	Nil.
"	10.12.16 1 am		MARCHEVILLE and STYLE — S.A.A.K. D.A.C. and reserve of petrol cartridges to 17 Lancers. Seals: 11 boxes S.A.A.K. D.A.C.	Nil.

WAR DIARY or INTELLIGENCE SUMMARY.

Army Form C. 2118.

Place	Date	Hour	Summary of Events and Information	Remarks and references to Appendices
PINCHE FALISE	11.12.16	8:45am	Car A1539 to ST VALERY for oil motor lorries & O.C. R.H.A. for about one week	
"	12 "	8 am	Box lorry t/c Car A/C to O.C. 61st Bd[n] at BOISMONT for duty	
"	13 "	1.30p	P.C. Hales A/C to Lieutenant N.O. MOYENVILLE to load ordnance & Box	M.C.
"	"		REPLY sent in	
"	"	3.45	Saloon lorries & supp till A.S.C. to QUESNOY to pick up staff. A. FORT REMY arr'd 7.30	
"	"		Jacobs area	
"	"	4p	1 CYCLE Hamer A.S.C. to ACHEUX to pick up letter [for] arm station	
"	"		Wilde	
"	"		2 lorries 1/c 2 Cpl Gardiner to BOISMONT	
"	"	4 "	1 left " Nittle C Field Amb.	
"	"	4.30	2 lorries 1/c 1 Cpl Humble to BOISMONT	
"	"		1 left " Goddard " luncheon Bag	
"	"		1 lorry 1/c Pte Cook ride to BOISMONT	
"	"		A.S.C. Field Sqdn Sialant Cycle	M.C.
"	"		" " " been to report to 2/Cavalry A.C. at FORT REMY and joined for duty	
"	"		" " " at foreword warmed point Archives C.du B. Flu detailed one left to intelligence	
"	"		Patrol Q 4932 4/12/14/16 on A.S.C. at Q5. W Bg at Boisemont	
"	"		Six lorries	
ABBEVILLE	14	3pm	Six lorries to MINWAY [illegible] pt. 7 K.D. Cherent	
"	"		" " Cullen A/C to QUESNOY " — "	
"	"		Two " " 40Pr Clark A/C to ORTHOU " — " 35 Jacob Annal	
"	"		" " " L. Lc	
"	"		Sheeming to transport Non. Spurten Salicit Rife from Bitca SATA	
PINCHE FALISE	15	7.45a	One lorry Cpl 4Pr Davidson to Field Squaron at BOISMONT thence to MONDICOURT	M.C.

WAR DIARY or INTELLIGENCE SUMMARY

Army Form C. 2118.

Place	Date	Hour	Summary of Events and Information	Remarks and references to Appendices
ANCHEFALISE	16/2/24	7 AM	Tudor Arrived I/c 2/Lt Cooke A.S.C with 840 ors 18 prs to D.A.C (FRESENNY)(?-L-?) Men to finish up from D.A.C. 849 ments dues and thence to No 12 Ordnance Depot at BLARGIES Exchange same for 3276 rounds 13 pr. on return from Blargies 1320 rounds to D.A.C. and 1056 rounds to Q Battery R.H.A at SAULEUSE near BLANGY and brought back as first Q ammunition establishment of Q Battery with 2 days of park 960 rounds.	MSC
	19m	7.15AM	Sarr Lewis I/c Sgt Gubbins etc to RE Dump MOINCOURT etc 10 from up Q RASRIEAE Echelon and then then to BLANGY proceeding to St HARRY Co at MACHY	MSC
	"	8 AM	One Lorry Q 4/Cpt Donaldson to report for duty to OC Tait Syndicate at BOISMONT thence to MOUDICOURT	
	18"	11 AM	Lorries Q 4/Cpt Harris etc to MOINCOURT to take up Loads attached to Cad Bde Supply Col to Le TREPORT	PSC
			Bre Tempo (Lewis) SGT & Cpl BARRETT	
	19 "	4 PM	Three Lorries I/c Cpl Vernon etc to ADDEVILLE BPK to MINMAY Return to BASE to AZ 6. 4/22 of 17/2/92	MSC
			Three Lorries I/c Sgt Gurr etc to MIANAY(?) Return hauling Infantry Huts	
	20"	9:15AM	One Lorry Q 4/Cpl Adams to BOISMONT for duty under orders of OC Tait Syndicate	
			4/Cpt Donaldson to report to R.O.C. B.O signalm and return to MOUCOURT	
			Three to St Blimer MC to MINMAY thence on to park of K.O.D.0 to ABBEVILLE	
	"	"	to hang forward	

WAR DIARY
or
INTELLIGENCE SUMMARY.

Army Form C. 2118.

Place	Date	Hour	Summary of Events and Information	Remarks and references to Appendices
ANCHEAPOLISE	22.12.16	8.45AM	Conv 1st R.A. Park to report to Asst D.A.D.S.+T. + Move to MOLLIENS AU BOIR (MIL Endg) @ 3646A. 30 park	MLC
"	23."	-	Visit to detailed situation VADENCOURT	MLC
"	24."	7.10AM	2nd/Lieut Aspinas to report to O/C ST VALERY & reports HQ 2nd Div Rev at MOYENNEVILLE	MLC
"	"	12 noon	Inspection of lorries & armament of convoy	
"	25."	-	Army routine	
"	26."	"	Army routine	MLC
"	27."	1 PM	Jon Bridge St Iva ASC to K.S.O. Ordnance Depot @ BLARGIES with 3/T empty R.P. lines & report	
"	"	2 PM	2nd Lieut Fields to Proceed to 2 Rly Cav Fd. Amb there two empty lorries and return with Sick and	
"	"	7 PM	wounded. 1st Lt. to return to R.P.C. at 3.30 pm as 2 Py Cav.	MLC
"	28."	8 PM	Ordnance 1/c 4 Cpl Holland to report to Capt Commandant DIVNARY	
"	"	-	Cav Dun for instructions. O/C Instruction + BOIRMONT. t Nour-N NOIRDICOURT + BOUGNERAILLE to take up 18/12 duties	MLC
"	29."	7 PM	Serion home 1/c CSM Pritchard ASC to @ Bakery R.H.A. @ SILLEVELLE to obtain some	MLC
"	"	8.15AM	and ½ trace to BLARGIES (No 10 ORDNANCE DEPOT) 4Cpl Asmus ASC to report to O/C Corps Troops Supply Column and to	MLC
"	"	-	Bakery 1/c 4Cpl Asmus ASC to 2rd Lieut for lorries for duty in Anticipating return to Div + 2 lorries Callfr remain. Light Contact party + ESCARDOTIN the 31st inst and to Parade w/t 2 Pink Cabs	
"	"	-	MOYENNEVILLE w/ 30½ unit No G37 D/28/12)	MLC
"	30."	-	Adj ASC 4 Cav Div No G37	
"	31."	8 AM	One adm 1/c 4Cpl Hamilton to report to O/C Field System @ BOIRMONT + Move to REGNIERE ECLUSE	MLC
"	"	"	Mour to MONDICOURT	MLC
"	"	-	Convoy 1/c 4Cpl Donaldson	

W.H. [signature], CAPTAIN ASC
O.C. 4TH CAVALRY DIVISIONAL AMMUNITION PARK

SERIAL NO. 146.

Confidential
War Diary
of

4TH CAVALRY DIVISIONAL AMMUNITION PARK.

FROM 1st JANUARY 1917. 1916 TO 31st JANUARY 1917. 1916

Army Form C. 2118.

WAR DIARY
or
INTELLIGENCE SUMMARY.
(Erase heading not required.)

Instructions regarding War Diaries and Intelligence Summaries are contained in F.S. Regs., Part II. and the Staff Manual respectively. Title pages will be prepared in manuscript.

Place	Date	Hour	Summary of Events and Information	Remarks and references to Appendices
PINCHEFALSE	1917 June		"ROUTINE"	
"	12/1/17		" "	W.F.I
"	13th		"ROUTINE". Re arming of RHA Bde 4th Cavalry Division with 13 pr Ammunition 17 lorries forwarded	W.F.I.
"	14th		to No 12 Ordnance Depôt at Dieu and distributed. The Ammunition required	W.F.I
"	15th & 26th		"ROUTINE" Frosty weather. All reductors inspected requiring new after coat antifreeze oily. No frost	W.F.I
"	"		Casualties	
"	27/1/17		A.D. of S&T Cavalry Corps inspected Company. Expressed his satisfaction. No frost casualties.	W.F.I
"	28/1/17		"Routine"	W.F.I.
"	29/1/17		"Routine"	W.F.I.
"	30/1/17		"ROUTINE" Inspection of unit by O.C. 4th Cavalry Divnl Amm Park who expressed himself satisfied with everything.	W.F.I.
"	31/1/17	noon	"ROUTINE".	W.F.I.

[signature]
O 4th Cavalry Divnl Ammunition Park

[stamp: 79 (M.T.) Co. A.S.C. 4TH CAV. DIVL AMMN PARK 31/1/17]

Army Form C. 2118.

Serial No. 146

WAR DIARY
or
INTELLIGENCE SUMMARY.
(Erase heading not required.)

Instructions regarding War Diaries and Intelligence Summaries are contained in F. S. Regs., Part II. and the Staff Manual respectively. Title pages will be prepared in manuscript.

WAR DIARY
—OF—

4th Cavalry Divisional Ammunition Park

For Month of February 1917

[signature]
O. 4th Cavalry Divl. Ammunition Park.

Place	Date	Hour	Summary of Events and Information	Remarks and references to Appendices

Army Form C. 2118.

WAR DIARY
or
INTELLIGENCE SUMMARY.
(Erase heading not required.)

Instructions regarding War Diaries and Intelligence Summaries are contained in F. S. Regs., Part II and the Staff Manual respectively. Title pages will be prepared in manuscript.

Place	Date	Hour	Summary of Events and Information	Remarks and references to Appendices
PONCHEFALISE	1-2-17		Routine.	
"	2 "		"	
"	3 "		"	
"	4 "		"	
"	5 "		"	
"	6 "		"	
"	7 "		"	
"	8 "		"	
"	9 "		"	
"	10 "		"	
"	11 "		"	
"	12 "		"	
"	13 "		"	
"	14 "		"	
"	15 "		"	
"	16 "		"	

Army Form C. 2118.

WAR DIARY
or
INTELLIGENCE SUMMARY.
(Erase heading not required.)

Instructions regarding War Diaries and Intelligence Summaries are contained in F. S. Regs., Part II. and the Staff Manual respectively. Title pages will be prepared in manuscript.

Place	Date	Hour	Summary of Events and Information	Remarks and references to Appendices
PINCHEFALISE	17·2·17		Routine	
"	18·2·17		" . Thaw Scheme (reference Q4995 d/19·12·16) (part in operation AwKy Q5575 and 9CAFC 4 Cav Div No 458 d/18/2/17	
"	19·2·17		Routine. Visited detailed subsection near MEAULTE.	
"	20·2·17		" . Temp² ²/Lieut R.S.C. Ward ASC struck off strength on Medical Certificate on form 13/2/17 Authority QMG. A.H.Q No ASC/14235 and 127603/9 d/13·2·17	M.C.
"	21·2·17		Routine	
"	22 "		"	
"	23 "		"	
"	24 "		"	
"	25 "		"	
"	26 "		" . Fire Service ¼c R.S.M Sale R.H.A. detached to No 2 Australian Sub-Park (CARCAILLOT FARM) for service of "A" Battery R.H.A Authority Q5652 4 Cav Div d/26·2·17 and Signal 1st RHA Qr Service and relief instructions Q 1 ANZAC CORPS d/26/2/17)	M.C.
"	27 "		Routine	
"	28 "		Routine	

Army Form C. 2118.

WAR DIARY
or
INTELLIGENCE SUMMARY. 14
(Erase heading not required.)

Serial No. 146.

WAR DIARY
OF
4TH CAVALRY DIVISIONAL AMMUNITION PARK
FOR MONTH OF MARCH 1917

Army Form C. 2118.

WAR DIARY
or
INTELLIGENCE SUMMARY.
(Erase heading not required.)

Instructions regarding War Diaries and Intelligence Summaries are contained in F. S. Regs., Part II. and the Staff Manual respectively. Title pages will be prepared in manuscript.

Place	Date	Hour	Summary of Events and Information	Remarks and references to Appendices
PUCHEVILLERS	1.3.17		Routine	
"	2 "		"	
"	3 "		"	
"	4 "		"	
"	5 "		Detachment of Gun Section consisting "A" Batty R.H.A. ½ R.U.H. Sub. L. R.H.A. moved to BONNEVILLE and	M.L.
"	6 "		inoculated war bakery	M.L.
"	7 "		Routine	
"	8 "		"	
"	9 "		"	
"	10 "		Above detachment proceeds to ST OUEN. Routine	
"	11 "		Routine. Same detachment proceeds to FIENVILLERS and is now attached to 13th Corps Ammn Park	M.L.
"	12 "		"	
"	13 "		"	
"	14 "		"	

WAR DIARY
INTELLIGENCE SUMMARY

Army Form C. 2118.

Place	Date	Hour	Summary of Events and Information	Remarks and references to Appendices
PUCHEVILLERS	14/3/17		Detachment of Gun Section i/c Lt Stacey RFA proceeded to Hd Qrs 4th Corps DAK.	M.B.C.
"	15 "		Routine. Lt. Stacey RFA proceeded to take over charge of detachment of Gun Section serving "A" Battery RHA	M.B.C.
"	16 "		Routine	"
"	17 "		"	"
"	18 "		" Detachment serving "A" Battery proceeded forward to points at front N.E. of C.S. Sheet 57 C.	M.B.C.
"	19 "		Three lorries of ammunition for R.I.M. late RHA proceeded to BAPAUME and dumped at point H 27 A 75. 22 units RR and 675 rds M.G. proceeded to Q 5 Corps. Remaining two lorries and one supply Column lorry proceeded to PUCHEVILLERS to replenish ammunition returning to Hd Qrs Q 5 Corps.	M.B.C.
"	20 "	8 am	Park & Gun above detachment serving "A" Batty proceeded to and parked at FIFFES — route via ASSEVILLERS, ST RIQUIER, BERNAVILLE and after arrival collected from Div Supply Column all ammunition. Auth ?/??? of A.D.S.S.? 17/3/17 to ???/???	M.B.C.
"	21 "	8 am	Park moved to and parked at point ½ mile N.W. of ALBERT on main ALBERT–BOUZINCOURT road. Auth O.C. A.S.C. of Corps Ref M/20/3/17.	M.B.C.
"	22 "		Returning prisoners collected from Div hunts to Railhead NIPPER MINE.	M.B.C.
"	23 "	3·30pm	Detachment of Gun Section armed with "A" Batty j/c Lt Stacey RFA rejoined Hdqrs from Batty 4th Corps Div Hqrs L/23/3/17	M.B.C.

WAR DIARY or INTELLIGENCE SUMMARY

Army Form C. 2118.

(Erase heading not required.)

Place	Date	Hour	Summary of Events and Information	Remarks and references to Appendices
Field	24-3-17		Routine. Key not available, made tool.	
"	25-3-17		One motor cart trailer WD No T.187 received from 3rd Auxiliary Petrol Company (Austerity DGT)	
"	"		No 47478 d/10/3/17) taken on establishment.	
"	26-3-17		9903 rds Market Hartley delivered to "A" Battery R.H.A. in action. Dump of 9003 rds 13pr in BAPAUME cleared	
"	"		by section of DAC. (A"/152g). 13pr delivered to BAPAUME as follows. 1216 rds. when dump was generated from DAC	
			in action.	
"	27-3-17		Routine. 95.2 rds "N" 338 rds "HE" issued ahead of horses to DAC in action in reply to 27th & 28th	
"	28-3-17		Dump at BAPAUME increased to 2000 rds as follows "N" 1507 rds. "HE" 500 Austerity N.C.B.A 300	
"	"		6/23/3/17 "R. I Corps"). 17 rds "H.E.", 338 rds "N". issued ahead of horses to DAC in action. Very bad	
			weather. Roads almost impassable.	
"	29-3-17		Routine. Road at BAPAUME closed to traffic. New conditions complete. Very bad weather. Wet & windy.	
"	30/3/17		"	
"	2/3/17		Routine. "	
			13pr. Dump at BAPAUME cleared.	

M.Forrest Capt
O.C.
79 Coy Dir Ammunition Park

2353 Wt. W254/...70 A.D.S.S./Forms/C. 2118.

Army Form C. 2118.

Serial No: 140.

WAR DIARY
or
INTELLIGENCE SUMMARY.
(Erase heading not required.)

WAR DIARY

OF

4TH CAVALRY DIVISIONAL AMMUNITION PARK.

FOR

MONTH OF APRIL 1917.

WAR DIARY
or
INTELLIGENCE SUMMARY.
(Erase heading not required.)

Army Form C. 2118.

Place	Date	Hour	Summary of Events and Information	Remarks and references to Appendices
Field.	1/4/17		Routine. Detained 10,000 rds of 13 pr Ammunition to the Divisional Ammunition Column at ACHIET LE GRAND in order to complete roads my text.	W.A.T.
"	"			
"	2/4/17		Routine. Drew up ammunition from O.W. and A.T. to complete to establishment. Unloaded my text & settling. Roads up text.	W.A.T.
"	3/4/17		Routine. 5 stories a with fatigues. Ammunition being sent up of by road to ACHIET-LE-GRAND Lorries not prepared for this.	W.A.T.
"	"		The moment my text on order	
"	4/4/17		Routine. 5 stories & road-repairing. My text & cold weather. Roads up text.	W.A.T.
"	5.4.17		Drew 31 pdr Ammn. Pistol Webley and explosives from O.Z.W.	B.C.B.
"	6.4.17		Routine. Drew from O.W. S.A.A. and grenades. Sent to ACHIET-LE-GRAND to draw ammn. 18 petrol dumps (Colins) Lieutenant. F.C. BEGG joined from M.T. Schools, Sanatorium, St. OMER. Q.M.G.H.Q. A.S.C. 15233 26.3.17	B.C.B.
"	7.4.17		Routine. 21 lorries took Ammn. to forward dumps for A.H.T. returned to D.A.C. dumps, and 13 lorries with 13/pdr for Corps.	B.C.B.
"	"		Dump proceeded to ACHIET-le-PETIT. 18 thank the night.	
"	8.4.17		Routine. 18 lorries proceeded to forward dump with ammn. returned D.A.C. and moved dump from there to Corps. Corps dump. Total amount dumped (Corps Corps dump). 9768.N. 2930.NX. 100000 S.A.A. 500 grenades N°3. A.H.T. dump counted :- 2024.N. 675.NX. 585,000 S.A.A. and 1800 grenades N°5. A.H.T. dump completed.	B.C.B.
"	9.4.17		Routine. 750,000 S.A.A. drawn from ALDWORTH.	B.C.B.

Army Form C. 2118.

WAR DIARY
or
INTELLIGENCE SUMMARY.
(Erase heading not required.)

Instructions regarding War Diaries and Intelligence Summaries are contained in F. S. Regs., Part II. and the Staff Manual respectively. Title pages will be prepared in manuscript.

Place	Date	Hour	Summary of Events and Information	Remarks and references to Appendices
Field	10.4.17		Routine. 1052 N.X, 1052 N, & 512 Shares No 7 Amm. ALDWORTH. Allrd @ Corps Dump.	
	11.4.17		304 Br. Abund Is D.A.C. 508 N.X. Remounts brought back to Park.	3.C.B
			Routine. The Park moved to B.5 HAGNIES arriving 2.30 P.M. Sun 2058 N.X 992 N. Ammuns 833 N X to Corps Dump. Remounts brought back to Park	3.C.B
	12.4.17		Routine. Snow thereby completing dump 15 14.600 Rounds 13/pr.	3.C.B
	13.4.17		Routine. R/s. in helmet and box respirators Inspection at 2.30.	3.C.B
	14.4.17		Routine. Weather as last issue.	3.C.B
	15.4.17		Routine. The Park moved to Sapignies arriving at 11.55. 76m. Weather dull.	J.J
	16.4.17		Routine. 176 N.X. 356 N 552 Pistol Webley issued to D.A.C. Weather fine.	J.J
	17.4.17		Routine. All Ammn dumped, 25 Lorries proceeded to Achiet le Grand for the purpose of unloading Ammn and conveying same to dumps at Louilleurs under orders of O.C. V Corps Ammn Park -: 3640 Rounds of 4.5 and 2640, 18pr.	J.J
	"		Routine. 8 Lorries proceeded to Miraumont under orders of V Corps to collect 412 Rounds of "D" and "Q.X." and convey same to B. 24. C. Sheet 57 C 12 miles E. of Merry. 6 Lorries proceeded to Miraumont to collect 511 Rounds of 60 pr. Ammn returned to Park at 11 pm with same.	J.J

WAR DIARY
or
INTELLIGENCE SUMMARY.
(Erase heading not required.)

Army Form C. 2118.

Place	Date	Hour	Summary of Events and Information	Remarks and references to Appendices
Field	18.4.17 (Contd)		6 Lorries proceeded to Achiet Le Grand under orders of V Corps for the purpose of collecting 500 Rds of "DX" 39 Bzes of Chargers and 493 Rds 60.PR. also 6 Lorries proceeded to Armament to collect 619 "DX" "58 D" 909 Bantridges 626 DA Fuzes Y.T.P. Fuzes and 449 Tubes and convey same to 19th Heavy Bty (Auth) No.114 d/17.17 O.C. "O" Corps Amm Park. (The foregoing during active operations.)	J.L. J.L. J.L.
Field	19.4.17		Routine. Lorries proceeded with 500 "DX" 39 Bzes of Chargers and 500 Rds Heavy Bty R.G.A. in Action (Clark) No 15 and 12 d/18/17 O.C. "O" Corps Amm Park. Empty cartridge cases (13 PR) collected to Railhead. 12 Lorries to Achiet Le Grand from D.A.C. and returned. 1852 to Behagnies Dump and collected 2332 "A.X." delivered 1852 to Behagnies Dump and 480 to Ervillers Dump. (Active Operations). Weather and Roads bad.	J.L. J.L.
-"-	20.4.17		Routine. Weather Fine.	J.L.
-"-	21.4.17		Routine. 14 Lorries proceeded to Achiet Le Grand to draw 1290 Rounds of "D" (60 PR). 611 Rds delivered to 19th H.B. dump at	J.L.

Army Form C. 2118.

WAR DIARY
or
INTELLIGENCE SUMMARY:
(Erase heading not required.)

Instructions regarding War Diaries and Intelligence Summaries are contained in F. S. Regs., Part II. and the Staff Manual respectively. Title pages will be prepared in manuscript.

Place	Date	Hour	Summary of Events and Information	Remarks and references to Appendices
Field	20.4.17 (Contd)		Behagnies and 589 Rds to 112th H.B. dumps at Ervillers (Active operation) Also Lorries were ordered to proceed to 19th H.B. dump at Behagnies and convey 60 PR Amn from there to the Battery in Action. (Auth) O.C. "O" Corps Amn Park. No W.2269 d/21.4.17. Weather fine and warm. Roads good.	JL
-"-	22.4.17		Routine. 19 Lorries were ordered to proceed to 19th H.B. Dump at Behagnies and convey 60 PR Amn from there to the Bty in Action (Auth) O.C. "O" Corps Amn Park No W 2245 d/21.4.17. Weather still fine.	JL
-"-	23.4.17		Routine. Weather fine. Roads very good.	JL
-"-	24.4.17		Routine. 10 Lorries were ordered to proceed to Monument Railhead to draw 666.B.C.B.R. and 450.B.S.H. (Gas Shells) and convey same to Behagnies Dumps (Active Operations) (Auth) O.C. "O" Corps Amn Park No W 2289 d/24.4.17. Weather still fine.	JL
-"-	25.4.17		Routine. 2 Lorries were ordered to proceed to Monument Railhead and draw 12,000 Rds Rifle Wet amtn 3,000 No 24	JL

WAR DIARY or INTELLIGENCE SUMMARY

Army Form C. 2118.

Place	Date	Hour	Summary of Events and Information	Remarks and references to Appendices
Field	25.4.17	(Cont'd)	Grenades & 1000 Stokes Cartridges (Green) and convey same to Corps Dumps at the Suerine Bihucourt (Auth) O.C. "O" Corps Amm. Park No W 2292 d/25.4.17. Weather fine. Roads very good.	J.S.
-"-	26.4.17		Routine. 3 lorries were ordered to proceed to Achiet Le Grand to draw 6.12 Rds of 18.Pr and convey same to Monument Railhead (Auth) O.C. "O" Corps Amm Park No 2303 d/26.4.17. Also 1 lorry collected 70 Rds of 60 Pr H.E. from 119th H.B. and conveyed same to 112th H.B. (in action) (Auth) O.C. "O" Corps Amm Park No.W. 2304 d/26.4.17.	J.S. J.S. J.S.
-"-	27.4.17		Routine. Weather fine.	
-"-	28.4.17		Routine.	
-"-	29.4.17		Routine. 12 lorries were ordered to proceed to Monument Railhead for the purpose of collecting 800 Rds of "D" and 300 "D.X." and deliver same to 119th H.B. (in action) (Auth) O.C. "O" Corps Amm Park No W 2314 d/29.4.17. Also 4 lorries collected 1200 3" Stokes French Mortar Amn, 1200 Green Cartridges, and 10,000 Pistol Webley, from Monument Railhead	J.S.

Army Form C. 2118.

WAR DIARY
or
INTELLIGENCE SUMMARY.
(Erase heading not required.)

Instructions regarding War Diaries and Intelligence Summaries are contained in F. S. Regs., Part II and the Staff Manual respectively. Title pages will be prepared in manuscript.

Place	Date	Hour	Summary of Events and Information	Remarks and references to Appendices
Field	29.4.17 (Contd)		and conveyed same to the Divisional Behrevsort (?) O.C. "D" Corps Amm. Park No. W. 2321 d/ 29.4.17. Weather still fine. Roads very good.	
-"-	30.4.17		Nothing. Weather fine and warm.	

W. Howard Capt.
O.C. 4th Cavalry Divisional Ammunition Park.

Army Form C. 2118.

WAR DIARY
or
INTELLIGENCE SUMMARY.
(Erase heading not required.)

Serial No: 146.

WAR DIARY
FOR MONTH ENDING MAY-17

From 1st May to 30th June 1917

Whitworth Capt.
for
O.C. 2 Cav. Div. Amm. Park.

79 (M.T) Co. A.S.C.
3/5/17
4TH CAV. DIV. AMMN. PARK

WAR DIARY or INTELLIGENCE SUMMARY

Army Form C. 2118.

Place	Date	Hour	Summary of Events and Information	Remarks and references to Appendices
Field	1.5.19		Routine. 13 Lorries were ordered to proceed to Monument Railhead for the purpose of drawing 1213 Rounds of 60 Pr and sent to Batteries on the following proportions:- 238 D and 169 DX to 112 HB. 238 D and 166 DX to 119th Battery and 237 D and 169 DX to 19th Battery including the amounts of Cartridges Fuzes and Tubes. (Active Operations) (Auth) O.C. "O" Corps Amm Park No.W. 2335 d/1.5.19. Fine weather continues	J1
-"-	2.5.19		Routine. 14 Lorries out on duty under orders of O.C. "O" Corps Amm Park No 87 d/1.5.19. Also 2 Lorries proceeded with 236 "N" 112 NX from Park to Q Battery R.H.A. (in Action) Weather fine and warm	J1
-"-	3.5.19		Routine. 16 Lorries on duty under orders of O.C. "O" Corps Amm Park (Auth) No 90 d/2.5.19 Also 6 Lorries proceeded from Park to Q Btty R.H.A. with 1084 "N" and 288 N.X and 4 Lorries to "J" Bty R.H.A. with 446 "N" and 601 "N.X" (In Action) Weather still fine	J1
-"-	4.5.19		Routine. 4 Lorries were ordered to proceed to the (Lucerne) Mailly Maillet and draw 480 Rds of "B.X" and deliver	J1

WAR DIARY
or
INTELLIGENCE SUMMARY.

(Erase heading not required.)

Army Form C. 2118.

Place	Date	Hour	Summary of Events and Information	Remarks and references to Appendices
Field	4.5.19 (Contd)		same to Behagnies Dump (Active Operations) Auth O.C. "O" Corps Amm Park d/3.5.19 also 13 lorries were detailed for duty under orders of O.C. "O" Corps Amm Park.	JS
"	5.5.19		Routine. 10 lorries on duty under orders of O.C. "O" Corps Amm Park, also 4 lorries proceeded to Achiet le Grand Railhead to draw 250 "D" 150 "D.X." and deliver to 119 L. H.B. (in action) (Auth) O.C. "O" Corps Amm Park. No. W.236 d/ 5.5.19.	JS
"	6.5.19		Routine 18 lorries on duty under orders of O.C. "O" Corps Amm Park. Weather cold and unsettled.	JS
"	7.5.19		Routine. 19 lorries on duty under orders of O.C. "O" Corps Amm. Park	JS
"	8.5.19		Routine. 19 lorries on duty under orders of O.C. "O" Corps Amm Park. Weather wet and cold.	JS
"	9.5.19		Routine. 21 lorries proceeded to "X.O." Amn Railhead to draw 4,900 Rds of "A" and deliver same to Behagnies tramway Dumps (Active Operations) (Auth) O.C. "O" Corps Amm Park No.W.2399 d/8.5.19. also 6 lorries on duty under orders of O.C. "O" Corps Amm. Park	JS

WAR DIARY
or
INTELLIGENCE SUMMARY.
(Erase heading not required.)

Army Form C. 2118.

Place	Date	Hour	Summary of Events and Information	Remarks and references to Appendices
Field	10/5/17		Routine. All available lorries were detailed under orders of O.C. 16th Brigade R.H.A. to return all amn. from Bazely Corps Dump, A.H.T. Dump and Amn. Park to X.B Corps Railhead and O Corps Dump at Behaucourt respectively. The total amn. consisted of the following :— 9,280 Rds of "N.X." 300 Rds 3 Pr. 2,459,000 Rds of S.A.A. 7,236 Grenades No 5 also 4,320 Empty 13 Pr. Boxes with clips and 1,574 Boxes and 860 empty 13 Pr. Boxes (Active Operations)	J
---	11/5/17		Routine. All available lorries on duty on continuation of above. Removal and return of all amn. completed by 12 noon the total number of lorry loads were 88.	
---	12/5/17		Routine. Park received orders to move leaving SAPIGNIES at 8.30 am arrived at a point ½ mile S.W. of Moreuve where lorries were parked fine weather continues	J
---	13/5/17		Routine.	J
---	14/5/17		Routine.	J

WAR DIARY or INTELLIGENCE SUMMARY

Army Form C. 2118.

(Erase heading not required.)

Place	Date	Hour	Summary of Events and Information	Remarks and references to Appendices
Field	15.3.17		Routine.	JS.
"	16.3.17		Routine.	JS.
"	17.3.17		Routine. 8 Lorries were detailed for duty under orders of O.C. A.S.C. Park ordered to move arriving at Chuignolles 32½ miles S.E. of Bray sur Somme at 2.50 p.m. where lorries were parked. Weather cold and wet.	JS.
"	18.3.17		Routine. 9 Lorries detailed for duty under orders of A.D. of S. & T. Cambridge.	JS.
"	19.3.17		Routine. 21 " " " " " " " " "	JS.
"	20.3.17		Routine. 14 " " " " " " " " "	JS.
"	21.3.17		Routine. 14 " " " " " " " " "	JS.
"	22.3.17		Routine. 9 " " " " " " " " "	JS.
"	23.3.17		Routine. 14 " " " " " " " " " Weather wet.	JS.
"	24.3.17		Routine. 10 " " " " " " " " " Weather fine.	JS.
"	25.3.17		Routine. 14 " " " " " " " " "	JS.
"	26.3.17		Routine. 14 " " " " " " " " "	JS.
"	27.3.17		Routine.	JS.

Army Form C. 2118.

WAR DIARY
or
INTELLIGENCE SUMMARY.
(Erase heading not required.)

Instructions regarding War Diaries and Intelligence Summaries are contained in F. S. Regs., Part II. and the Staff Manual respectively. Title pages will be prepared in manuscript.

Place	Date	Hour	Summary of Events and Information	Remarks and references to Appendices
Field	28/5/17		Routine. 20 Lorries detailed for duty under orders of A.D. of S.&T. Cav. Corps.	JP
"	29/5/17		Routine. Park ordered to move arriving at a point ½ mile E. of FOUCAUCOURT 9.5 miles S.E. of BRAY-SUR-SOMME where lorries were Parked (Auth) Cav. Corps No 9 361. 21/28.17. Weather fine	JP
"	30/5/17		Routine. 20 Lorries detailed for duty under orders of A.D. of S.&T. Cav. Corps.	JP
"	31/5/17		Routine. 20 " " " " " " " " "	JP

O.C. 79 Cav Divn Amm Park

[Stamp: 79 (M.T.) Co. A.S.C. ☆ 4TH CAV. DIV. AMMN. PARK 31/5/17]

Army Form C. 2118.

WAR·DIARY.
or
INTELLIGENCE SUMMARY.

(Erase heading not required.)

Summary of Events and Information

WAR DIARY
For June 1917

H.R. Horan, Captain
O.C. 4th Cavalry Divisional Ammunition Park.

[Stamp: 79 (M.T) CO. A.S.C. — 4TH CAV. DIV. AMM. PARK — 30/6/17]

Instructions regarding War Diaries and Intelligence Summaries are contained in F. S. Regs., Part II. and the Staff Manual respectively. Title pages will be prepared in manuscript.

Place	Date	Hour		Remarks and references to Appendices

Army Form C. 2118.

WAR DIARY
or
INTELLIGENCE SUMMARY.
(Erase heading not required.)

Instructions regarding War Diaries and Intelligence Summaries are contained in F. S. Regs., Part II. and the Staff Manual respectively. Title pages will be prepared in manuscript.

Place	Date	Hour	Summary of Events and Information	Remarks and references to Appendices
Field	1.6.17	Routine	20 Lorries detailed for duty under orders of A.D.S.o.T. Base Corps.	JP
---	2.6.17	Routine	20 " " " " " " " " "	JP
---	3.6.17	Routine	20 " " " " " " " " "	JP
---	4.6.17	Routine	22 " " " " " " " " "	JP
---	5.6.17	Routine	22 " " " " " " " " "	JP
---	6.6.17	Routine	22 " Inspection of lorries by representative of Inspection Branch	JP
---	7.6.17	Routine	20 " detailed for duty under orders of A.D.S.o.T. Base Corps	JP
---	8.6.17	Routine	21 " " " " " " " " "	JP
---	9.6.17	Routine	21 " " " " " " " " "	JP
---	10.6.17	Routine	21 " " " " " " " " "	JP
---	11.6.17	Routine	21 " " " " " " " " "	JP
---	12.6.17	Routine	22 " " " " " " " " "	JP
---	13.6.17	Routine	21 " " " " " " " " "	JP
---	14.6.17	Routine	21 " " " under orders of R.E. & O.i.c. Convoys to Marquise	JP
---	15.6.17	Routine	20 " " " " " " " " "	JP
---	16.6.17	Routine	23 " " " " " " " " "	JP

Army Form C. 2118.

WAR DIARY
or
INTELLIGENCE SUMMARY.
(Erase heading not required.)

Instructions regarding War Diaries and Intelligence
Summaries are contained in F. S. Regs., Part II.
and the Staff Manual respectively. Title pages
will be prepared in manuscript.

Place	Date	Hour	Summary of Events and Information	Remarks and references to Appendices
Field	17/6/17		Routine. 23 Lorries detailed for duty under orders of A.D.S.&T. Cav. Corps	J.S.
"	18/6/17		Routine. 20. " " " " " "	J.S.
"	19/6/17		Routine. 20. " " " " " " also 1.	J.S.
"	"		Lorry detailed for duty since 9th inst. for carrying the Divisional Cinema (Auth) A.D.S.&T. Cav. Corps. No T/826 d/ 5.6.17	J.S.
"	20/6/17		Routine. 21 Lorries detailed for duty under orders of A.D.S.&T. Cav. Corps.	J.S.
"	21/6/17		Routine. 20. " " " " " "	J.S.
"	22/6/17		Routine. 20. " " " " " "	J.S.
"	23/6/17		Routine. 20. " " " " " "	J.S.
"	24/6/17		Routine. 20. " " " " " "	J.S.
"	25/6/17		Routine. 20. " " " " " "	J.S.
"	26/6/17		Routine. 21. " " " " " "	J.S.
"	27/6/17		Routine. 20. " " " " " " 326 T.C. Bigg admitted to Hospital	J.S.
"	28/6/17		Routine. 20. " " " " " " under orders of A.D.S.T. Cav. Corps.	J.S.
"	29/6/17		Routine. 20. " " " " " "	J.S.
"	30/6/17		Routine. 20. " " " " " "	J.S.

Army Form C. 2118.

WAR DIARY
or
INTELLIGENCE SUMMARY.
(Erase heading not required.)

Serial No. 146.

WAR DIARY.

JULY. 1917.

M. Grant Captain ASC.
O. C. 4th Cav Divl Ammtn Park.

Army Form C. 2118.

WAR DIARY
or
INTELLIGENCE SUMMARY.

(Erase heading not required.)

Instructions regarding War Diaries and Intelligence Summaries are contained in F. S. Regs., Part II. and the Staff Manual respectively. Title pages will be prepared in manuscript.

Place	Date	Hour	Summary of Events and Information	Remarks and references to Appendices
Field	1.7.17		Routine. 20 Lorries detailed for duty under orders of A.D.S.T. Cav. Corps	ff
"	2.7.17		Routine. 20 " " " " " "	ff
"	3.7.17		Routine. 21 " " " " " "	ff
"	4.7.17		Routine. 20 " " " " " "	ff
"	5.7.17		Routine. 20 " " " " " "	ff
"	-.7.17		2nd Lieut F.C. Begg A.S.C. rejoined from Hospital	ff
"	6.7.17		Routine. 20 Lorries detailed for duty under orders of A.D.S.T Cav. Corps	ff
"	7.7.17		Routine. 20 " " " " " "	ff
"	8.7.17		Routine. Park ordered to move to LE MESNIL 3 miles S.E. of PERONNE	ff
"	9.7.17		(Auth.) A.D.S.T. Cavalry Corps. No MT/143 d/4/7/17 Weather Bad	ff
"	10.7.17		Routine. 8 Lorries detailed for duty under orders of A.D.S.T Cav. Corps	ff
"			Routine. 8 Lorries detailed for duty conveying Ammunition from X.B Amtn Railhead to Bancourt Dumps (auth) Bav Corps No S.T.W.1619-1/7/17	ff
"	11.7.17		Routine 16 Lorries detailed for Ammunition Duty (auth) Cav Corps No S.T.W 1619 and Q.A.269 d/1.10.17, also 1 Lorry detailed for Bainleux d/1.10.17	ff
"	"		H.Q Mhow B2c (Auth) OC A.S.C. No 38, d/1.10.17	ff

WAR DIARY
or
INTELLIGENCE SUMMARY.

Army Form C. 2118.

(Erase heading not required.)

Instructions regarding War Diaries and Intelligence Summaries are contained in F. S. Regs. Part II. and the Staff Manual respectively. Title pages will be prepared in manuscript.

Place	Date	Hour	Summary of Events and Information	Remarks and references to Appendices
Field	12/7/17		Routine. 13 Lorries detailed for duty (Auth) O.C.A.S.C. No 2/10 $\frac{A}{281}$ d/11.7.17	J.L.
"	13/7/17		Routine. 14 Lorries detailed for various duties (Auth) A.D.S.T Bus Boylo Weather fine.	J.L.
"	14/7/17		No.T 756 " O.C.A.S.C. No A/296 dated 12.7.17. 1 Lorry detached for duty (Auth) O.C.A.S.C. No A/302 d/13.17	J.L.
"	15/7/17		Routine. 4 " " for various duties (Auth) O.C.A.S.C No 893 and Corr Boylo. No. 3.T.W 1619 d/14/7/17 1 Lorry attached to Divl Supply Column T 802	J.L.
"	16/7/17		since 9.6.17 returned to Park on completion of duty (Auth) A.D.S.T Bus Boylo No G.L. Routine. 2 Lorries detached for duty (Auth) O.C A.S.C No $\frac{A}{302}$ and 310 d/15.17	J.L.
"	17/7/17		Routine " " " " " " A/910 d/16.7.17	J.L.
"	18/7/17		Routine. 4 " " " " " " $\frac{A}{310}$ and 923 d/15.7 – 17/7/17	J.L.
"	19/7/17		Routine. 12 " " " " " " $\frac{A}{310}$ and 317 d/17.18/7/17	J.L.
"	20.7.17		Routine.	MSC
"	21.7.17		Routine.	MSC
"	22/7/17		Routine.	MSC
"	23/7/17		Routine. 2/Lt Stacey R.F.A with one NCO & 5 Gunners R.H.A. proceeded to MANCOURT to take charge of 13pr Sump Fire (Auth. 1633/1 D. 23/7/17 of Adj R.H.A Bgde.)	

WAR DIARY
or
INTELLIGENCE SUMMARY.

(Erase heading not required.)

Army Form C. 2118.

Place	Date	Hour	Summary of Events and Information	Remarks and references to Appendices
Field	24/7/17		Continue Issue from X.U. HAMEL 12960 rds Rifle Nobly, 7 issues same in Equal proportions to Brigades	MSR
"	25/7/17		"	MSR
"	26/7/17		"	MSR
"	27/7/17		"	MSR
"	28/7/17		"	MSR
"	29/7/17		Hrs Morris 1/c Sergt Guthier to X.U. HAMEL to draw 215000 rds S.A.A. and 2560 Grenades Rifle	MSR
"	30/7/17		No 20 and Notice to Div' Ammunition Col'n to delivering same	
"	31/7/17		Continue —	MSR

A.J. Howard, Captain A.S.C.
O.C. 4th Cavalry Division Ammunition Park

[Stamp: 79 (M.T) Co. A.S.C. 4TH CAV. DIV. AMMTN. PARK 31/7/17]

Army Form C. 2118.

WAR DIARY
or
INTELLIGENCE SUMMARY.
(Erase heading not required.)

Serial No: 146.

WAR DIARY
—FOR—
AUGUST 1917

W.R.

M. Harrap Capt
oc 79 Cavalry Divisional
Ammunition Park

79 (M.T) CO. A.S.C.
4TH CAV. DIV. AMMN. PARK

Army Form C. 2118.

WAR DIARY
or
INTELLIGENCE SUMMARY.
(Erase heading not required.)

Instructions regarding War Diaries and Intelligence Summaries are contained in F. S. Regs., Part II and the Staff Manual respectively. Title pages will be prepared in manuscript.

Place	Date	Hour	Summary of Events and Information	Remarks and references to Appendices
LE MESNIL	1917 Aug 1		Routine	
"	" 2		"	MSS
"	" 3		"	MSS
"	" 4		" Drew from XV Railhead 2160 rds Pistol Webley 450 Cartridges VI Rifle Grenades & other small arms and delivered same to D.A.C.	MSS MSS
"	" 5		Routine	
"	" 6		" Eleven horses & Mr Cutbertson with dismounted men & 29 Lancers & 6th Inniskillings transferred to VILLERS FAUCON	MSS
"	" 7		Horse to EPEHY and thence with party of Lancashire Fusiliers to VILLERS FAUCON	MSS
"	" 8		Routine	
"	" 9		Routine	
"	" 10		" Eight horses & Sgt Stott att'd to VILLERS FAUCON with No. 12 Machine Gun Squadron	MSS
"	" 11		"	
"	" 12		"	MSS
"	" 13		"	
"	" 14		"	MSS

Army Form C. 2118.

WAR DIARY
or
INTELLIGENCE SUMMARY.
(Erase heading not required.)

Instructions regarding War Diaries and Intelligence Summaries are contained in F. S. Regs., Part II. and the Staff Manual respectively. Title pages will be prepared in manuscript.

Place	Date	Hour	Summary of Events and Information	Remarks and references to Appendices
LE MESNIL	15.7.17		Routine. One lorry to O.O. "XII" Brigade 29,000 rds S.A.A. and 2160 Rifle Webley and fuze 80	R88
"	16.8.17		D.A.C. to column	R89
"	17 "		Routine	R90
"	18 "		"	R91
"	19 "		"	
"	20 "		"	R92
"	21 "		"	
"	22 "		"	
"	23 "		"	
"	24 "		"	
"	25 "		"	R93
"	26 "		"	
"	27 "		"	
"	28 "		"	
"	29 "		"	

Army Form C. 2118.

WAR DIARY
or
INTELLIGENCE SUMMARY.
(Erase heading not required.)

Place	Date	Hour	Summary of Events and Information	Remarks and references to Appendices
LE MESNIL	30.8.17	Routine		
"	31.8.17	"		

[Signature]
O.C. 4 Cavalry Divisional Ammunition Park
31. August 1917

Army Form C. 2118.

Serial No. 146

WAR DIARY
or
INTELLIGENCE SUMMARY.
(Erase heading not required.)

WAR DIARY
— FOR —
SEPTEMBER 1917

Instructions regarding War Diaries and Intelligence Summaries are contained in F. S. Regs., Part II. and the Staff Manual respectively. Title pages will be prepared in manuscript.

Army Form C. 2118.

WAR DIARY
or
INTELLIGENCE SUMMARY.
(Erase heading not required.)

Instructions regarding War Diaries and Intelligence Summaries are contained in F.S. Regs., Part II. and the Staff Manual respectively. Title pages will be prepared in manuscript.

Place	Date	Hour	Summary of Events and Information	Remarks and references to Appendices
LE MESNIL	1917 Sept 1		Routine	
"	2		"	MSC
"	3		T/2/Lieut H.G.W. Buckbridge posted to join this unit from M.T. School of Inst in lieu 1/2/Lt F.C. Bagg who is posted to Cav/Corps Troops Supply Column (Authority Q.M.G. GHQ No A/394 D. 30/5/17)	MSC
"	4		Routine	
"	5		"	MSC
"	6		Routine	
"	7		Drew from XV Railhead 1308 rts Branch 303 rations — delivered same to Divisional Units	MSC
"	8		"	
"	9		"	
"	10		Drew from XV Railhead 21600 rts Picket Winter and delivered 15600 rts to D.A.C. and 6000 rts to Lucknow Bgde	MSC
"	11		Routine	
"	12		Three lorries detached /c Cpl Clark A.S.C. to POZIERES Salvage Dump and twelve lorries 1/c 2/Lt H.G.W. Buckbridge A.S.C. to MONTAUBAN Brigade Dump (Authority O.C. A.S.C. No A/394 D 9/9/17)	MSC
"	13		Routine. 2/Lt F.C. Bagg A.S.C. proceeded to join Cavalry Corps Troops Supply Column (Authority Q.M.G. G.H.Q. No A/394 10/33 — 10/33 - d/10/17)	

Army Form C. 2118.

WAR DIARY
or
INTELLIGENCE SUMMARY.
(Erase heading not required.)

Place	Date	Hour	Summary of Events and Information	Remarks and references to Appendices
Field	13th Sept		Routine. On Daimler lorry car and the Douglas motor Cycle to suspend at Second Army Troops Supply Column and D.A.T. (Section) necessitating a reduction of establishment. (Authority ADSS&T No. T.893 4/9/17)	MBE
"	14" "		Routine.	MBE
"	15-16 "		Routine.	MBC
"	16 "		Routine.	MBC
"	17 "		Routine.	MBC
"	18 "		Routine.	MBE
"	19 "		Routine.	MBE
"	20 "		Routine.	MBE
"	21 "		Routine.	MBE
"	22 "		Routine.	MBE
"	23 "		Routine.	MBE
"	24 "		Routine.	
"	25 "		Routine.	
"	26 "		Routine.	

Army Form C. 2118.

WAR DIARY
or
INTELLIGENCE SUMMARY.
(Erase heading not required.)

Instructions regarding War Diaries and Intelligence Summaries are contained in F. S. Regs., Part II. and the Staff Manual respectively. Title pages will be prepared in manuscript.

Place	Date	Hour	Summary of Events and Information	Remarks and references to Appendices
S. K. Park	Sep 27 1917	Routine		
"	" 28	Routine		
"	" 29	Routine		
"	" 30	Routine		

Army Form C. 2118.

(146)

WAR DIARY
or
INTELLIGENCE SUMMARY.
(Erase heading not required.)

WAR DIARY
FOR
OCTOBER 1917

4TH CAVALRY DIVISIONAL AMMUNITION PARK.

Place	Date	Hour	Summary of Events and Information	Remarks and references to Appendices

Army Form C. 2118.

WAR DIARY
or
INTELLIGENCE SUMMARY.
(Erase heading not required.)

Place	Date	Hour	Summary of Events and Information	Remarks and references to Appendices
In the field	1917 Oct 1		Routine	M&C
"	" 2	"	"	M&C / R&C
"	" 3	"	"	C&C
"	" 4	"	Park moves to point P.27 d central, sheet 62d. Authority O.C A.S.C 4 Cav¹ Div⁻	R&B
"	" 5	"	"	
"	" 6	"	"	
"	" 7	"	"	R&B
"	" 8	"	"	
"	" 9	"	"	
"	" 10	"	"	
"	" 11	"	"	R&C
"	" 12	"	"	
"	" 13	"	"	
"	" 14	"	"	
"	" 15	"	"	
"	" 16	"	"	

Army Form C. 2118.

WAR DIARY
or
INTELLIGENCE SUMMARY.
(Erase heading not required.)

Place	Date	Hour	Summary of Events and Information	Remarks and references to Appendices
D.H. fld	17/4/17		Continue.	MHC
"	18 "		" Drew from 24th Division Dump 1348 rds NX and 1352 rds N Authority H. Autwks II Rept Q.A. 117 D 15/4/17	MHC
"	19 "		" Capt H.J.M Howard ASC handed over command of this unit to Capt H.C. Howard ASC	MHC
"	20 "		in accordance with Cav. Corps G 2838 D/18/4/17 and GO ASC 4 Cavalry Dn. 10. 1/320 D 19.10.17 Routine. Capt H.J.M Howard and 2/Lt H.G.W. Burbidge proceeded with rnfts from MD & FMCOS. y	MHC
"	21 "		this unit to report to Commandant ABBEVILLE in accordance with above authority. Routine. Drew from 7th Corps Ammn Dump 685, rds no RAA 9936 Field W. 1 1805 Penetrative No 5.	MHC
"	22 "		to complete establishment Authority 3rd Corps No Q A 117 D/15:10/17	MHC
"	23 "		Routine	MHC
"	24 "		Routine	MHC
"	25 "		" Drew from GW Rail Hd. 900 Grenades rifle & handed same to Brigades	MHC
"	26 "		" Drew from XZ	MHC
"	27 "		" Drew from XZ 2/60 Cartridges SA Blank and issued same to Lucknow Bde. also above	MHC
"	27 "		from XV 600 Cartridges SAA & 300 rubber tube covers	
"	28 "		Routine Routine	MHC

Army Form C. 2118.

WAR DIARY
or
INTELLIGENCE SUMMARY.
(Erase heading not required.)

Instructions regarding War Diaries and Intelligence Summaries are contained in F. S. Regs., Part II. and the Staff Manual respectively. Title pages will be prepared in manuscript.

Place	Date	Hour	Summary of Events and Information	Remarks and references to Appendices
In the Field	29.10.17		Routine. Issued to 4 Cav. D.A.C. two Cartridges Sh. S various gun points &c.	ASC ASC ASC
"	30 "		Routine	
"	31 "		Routine	

J.P.Howard Capt ASC
O.C. 4th Cav Div Amm Park

146

WAR DIARY
-of-
4th Cavalry Divisional Ammunition Park
-for-
NOVEMBER 1917

Army Form C. 2118.

WAR DIARY
or
INTELLIGENCE SUMMARY.

(Erase heading not required.)

Instructions regarding War Diaries and Intelligence Summaries are contained in F. S. Regs., Part II. and the Staff Manual respectively. Title pages will be prepared in manuscript.

Place	Date	Hour	Summary of Events and Information	Remarks and references to Appendices
Field	1917 Nov. 1		Routine. Returned to "XU" 128 rds N + 4 rds NX (defective) rds corresponding recants.	MSE
"	" 2		"	MSE
"	" 3		Record of review Divisional units 25% of Mens establishment of explosives for exchange and obtained same to XU in exchange for similar quantity issued by same HQ.	MSE
"	" 4		Routine. Returned to Brittain Div Unit Mens proportions of explosives shown	MSE
"	" 5		Routine. Returned to remaining " except DAC when proportions were drawn from	MSE
"	" 6		"XB" 276 PAR Wthy 2 no coils fuse 61 box Cart. Sfg 9.	MSE
"	" 6		Routine. Received from DAC 25% of its establishment of explosives (in exchange for which extra explosive surplus to its establishment in return for 72 M. Bennetts, DAC 2 no rds	MSE
"	7		Round Cart P.M. + 1 box cart illuminating.	
"	8		Routine.	MSE
"	9		Routine.	MSE
"	10		Routine.	MSE
"	11		" Received of DAC 249 rds N unserviceable + issued in exchange corresponding number	MSE
"	12		" " 38,000 " SAA 224 Rifle Grenades No 20 + 24 ditto No 23 heavy surplus to 2/3	MSE

WAR DIARY
or
INTELLIGENCE SUMMARY

Army Form C. 2118.

Place	Date	Hour	Summary of Events and Information	Remarks and references to Appendices
In Field	12.11.17		Establishment & entrain. Stores from 36 Jacob three for exchange	MSE
"	13.11.17		Routine. Received from Div. dump uniforms Main establishment of Main Stores. Drew from XZ. Rhens. 1620 N 1050 NX 642,000 SAA 2500 vet flares and delivered same to 4th Cav A.H.T. Dv. as is establishment. Drew from XZ 9020 rifl flares & 50 Very light's green. Issued to + DAC 16000 SAA & to N 125 vet also T126 Q.S change also antim flares & Very lights and to Ds Sig R. Delivered to Ruin Amt Dump 549 vet defective	MSE
"	14.11.17		Routine. Drew from XV 328 vet N. Issued to Imperishable Dpre & Bt Cav 7 Maxims with 1st sheet of machine & auto & part vet & othr items	MSE
"	15.11.17		Routine. Drew from XZ 200 vet Regt (BLC Nol 3rd) & issued vet debts to Armd Offn Cav Cops	MSE
"	16.11.17		Surplus explosives returned to Park by River Raft & Dv's. Issued to 6 regiments flares red	MSE
"	17.11.17		Cartridges signal green & 0045 pistol & P.N. also to DAC springs magazines. Routine. Surplus rifle grenades received from 29 Lancers. Drew from XV 1008 P.N. 1620 SAA. Returned to XB all surplus explosives grenades	MSE
"	"		Ammn piercing 12 boxes Cart SAA + 76 vet N. Issued to 15th Machine Gun Squadt 18,000 SAA 20 ground flares red	
"	18."."		Routine. Received from 36 Jacobs Horse 2nd Lancers & 91 Jullpur Lancers + 38° C.I.H all surplus grenades & defective explosives. Issues of ammn 2(SA) + explosives to tree units	MSE

2353 Wt. W2544/1454 700,000 5/15 D.D.&L. A.D.S.S./Forms/C. 2118.

Army Form C. 2118.

WAR DIARY
or
INTELLIGENCE SUMMARY.
(Erase heading not required.)

Place	Date	Hour	Summary of Events and Information	Remarks and references to Appendices
Field	19.11.17		Routine. Dust from XZ various Staff Asst Colt Stares transferring also from K13 mill also various & demolition stores also from RUIN Grenades Hand. Lorries of atts to air Div. until 16. 22 lorries i/c 2/Lt Cooke still to MISERY where with Pioneer Battn 4 Cav. Div. to FINS	MSE
"	20.11.17		Routine. Dust from XZ Stores & SAA also Cartridges Signalling. Lorries of atts to 3 under Park moved to Point C20a 8.8. (Sh. 62c) LE TRANSLOY – BOUCHAVESNES road and came into harrant Capt. Spafford A/I/C. (Auth. DA & QMG Cav. Corps D 17/11/17)	MSE
"	21.11.17 22.11.17		Routine Four lorries i/c Cpl Turner to YTRES to report to Supply officer for duty returns to FINS. Three lorries i/c Sgt Clark to LA CHAPELETTE to report to ADOS Cav. Corps whence to METZ Sixteen lorries on Supply Column put pieces to Bois de TINCOURT and thence to RANCOURT	MSE MSE MSE
"	23.11.17		Five lorries i/c Cpl Stahl Smith to HQ A/I/C 4 Cav. Div. for duty in that area. Park moved to MONS EN CHAUSSEE	MSE
"	24.11.17		Routine	MSE
"	25.11.17		Four lorries i/c Sgt Clark to Q. Officer VILLERS CARBONNEL for duty. Twenty lorries i/c 2/Lt Cooke also to MISERY to meet Pioneer Battn 4 Cav. Div. to Billets	MSE
"	26.11.17		Routine	
"	27.11.17		"	MSE
"	28.11.17		"	MSE

Army Form C. 2118.

WAR DIARY
or
INTELLIGENCE SUMMARY.
(Erase heading not required.)

Instructions regarding War Diaries and Intelligence Summaries are contained in F. S. Regs., Part II. and the Staff Manual respectively. Title pages will be prepared in manuscript.

Place	Date	Hour	Summary of Events and Information	Remarks and references to Appendices
Field	29.11.17	Continue		
"	30.11.17	"		

J.R. Howard Capt ASC
O.C. 4th Cav Div Amm Park

Army Form C. 2118.

(146)

WAR DIARY
or
INTELLIGENCE SUMMARY.
(Erase heading not required.)

WAR DIARY
- OF -
4th CAVALRY DIVISIONAL AMMN PARK
- FOR -
DECEMBER 1917

Place	Date	Hour	Summary of Events and Information	Remarks and references to Appendices

Army Form C. 2118.

WAR DIARY
or
INTELLIGENCE SUMMARY.
(Erase heading not required.)

Instructions regarding War Diaries and Intelligence Summaries are contained in F.S. Regs., Part II. and the Staff Manual respectively. Title pages will be prepared in manuscript.

Place	Date	Hour	Summary of Events and Information	Remarks and references to Appendices
Fields O.S. d.6.2. Sheet 62C	1917 Dec 1	1. AM	Routine. Ten lorries 1/c 2/Lt Cooke ASC to deliver 1428 rds N and 1340 rds NX to MONTIGNY FARM	MSE
	" "	12 noon	Ten lorries to QUINCONCE to stand by	MSE
	" "	12.30 pm	2/Lt Cooke to HQ Cav Corps Ammn Park. 8 lorries with ammn to deliver 500 rds rds SAA to Cavalry Corps Advanced Ammn Dump at QUINCONCE E.15.a.0.3. Ry Siding 62C	MSE
	" "	1 pm	Two lorries to QUINCONCE to draw 380 rds N	MSE
	" "	5 pm	Eleven lorries & Capt Howard ASC to deliver 2010 rds N and 1000 rds NX to Cav Corps Advanced Dump at QUINCONCE about	MSE
	" 2	12.30 pm	Routine. 4 lorries (this park & 4 of 5th Can DAP) 1/c 2/Lt Cooke to Ammn dump with 1080 NX + 1040 N & Ammn up	MSE
	"	5 pm	Six lorries 1/c Officer 1/5 Can AP with 1620 rds N to ammn Cav Corps Dump, QUINCONCE	
	" 3		Routine returned from QUINCONCE	
	" 4	6 am	Two lorries 1/c Cpl Vinson to 59 Labour Coy, Detachment at BEUILLY returning to HAVECOURT with 59 personnel	
			Ten lorries 1/c 2/Lt Cooke ASC to deliver 1620 rds N and 1080 NX to Ammn Dump advanced	
		"	4 lorries to QUINCONCE drawing up ammn graduating	
	" 5	"	Two lorries to ATHIES for Divl Canteen duty	
	" 5	8 "	Routine	
	" 6	6.30 AM	Three lorries 1/c Cpl Vinson ASC to ARRAS to draw lorries from No 8 RE Park and thence to deliver same to 4th Cav Div. 1st Field Squadron at FOUQUES	
		7.15 am	Fourteen lorries 1/c 2/Lt Cooke to CRE Cavalry Corps at VILLERS FAUCON and thence to BRIE with white rc.	
	"	3 pm	Seven lorries 1st CAR Mow lorries 3rd CAP, 12 lorries 4th CAP and 2 lorries 5th CAP, 1/c Capt Howard ASC to LONGAVESNES to carry Korps Ammn from there to PERONNE	MSE

WAR DIARY
or
INTELLIGENCE SUMMARY.
(Erase heading not required.)

Army Form C. 2118.

Instructions regarding War Diaries and Intelligence Summaries are contained in F. S. Regs., Part II. and the Staff Manual respectively. Title pages will be prepared in manuscript.

Place	Date	Hour	Summary of Events and Information	Remarks and references to Appendices
Field	7.12.17	7 AM	Ten lorries ¹/c 2/Lt Crane ASC to Cross Roads Branch N.E. of LONGAVESNES to remove ammunition to mud dumps at MONTIGNY FARM	WSC
		12:30 pm	Eight Auxiliar lorries ¹/c Sgt Hearne on service duty	
"	8.12.17	6 AM	Five lorries ¹/c Sr Clerk to RE dump FOISAL to carry RE material belonging to 2⁴ᵈ Div² at MONTIGNY RE dump	WSC
			Three lorries ¹/c Cpl Vinson to RE dump FOISSY to carry timber to 2ⁿᵈ Cav Field Squadron at FOUEQUES	
			Three lorries ¹/c Cpl Smith to RE dump FROISSY to take timber to BRIE Rlwy dump 62ᵈ. short. Authority OC Cav Corps Amm" Park D7¹²/₁₇	
		9:15 am	Park moved to M 30.a.2.0 Reference to No C.A. 63	WSC
"	9.12.17		Routine.	WSC
"	10.12.17		Routine. All ammunition dumped – Auth ¹/₉ Cav Corps Amm" Pk D 10¹²/₁₇ No Q & PC	WSC
"	11.12.17		Routine. Thirteen lorries to Cross-roads dump NE of LONGAVESNES to collect S410 nts and Vx and dump same at this Park	WSC
"	12.12.17		Routine. This Park came under command of O.C. 4ᵗʰ Cavalry Div¹ Sup Col Admin as a Subparc pending return of that unit but remains transport detail only. Authority of OC Cav Corps Amm" Park for purposes of Transport detail only. AD 4 HT Cav Corps No P1153/8 D/9/17	WSC

J R Howard Capt ASC
O.C. 4ᵗʰ Cav Div Amm Park

[4TH CAVALRY DIVISIONAL AMMUNITION PARK stamp]